A Pocket Guide to **Snowdon**

The Snowdon Horseshoe from Llynnau Mymbyr

www.snowdoniamountains.co.uk

A Pocket Guide to *Snowdon*
Yr Wyddfa

R Russell Roberts

MARA BOOKS

www.marabooks.co.uk
www.northerneyebooks.co.uk

First published in September 2002 by **Mara Books**, 22 Crosland Terrace,
Helsby, Frodsham, Cheshire WA6 9LY. Telephone: 01928 723744

Second edition published July 2004.

Third edition published August 2007, reprinted August 2010.

ISBN: 978 1 902512 16 7

www.marabooks.co.uk
www.northerneyebooks.co.uk
www.snowdoniamountains.co.uk

Layout, mapping, design and photography by Carl Rogers.

Cover photos © Carl Rogers 2007
                      Front: Snowdon from the east looking into Cwm Dyli
                      Rear: Snowdon from the west

Text © R Russell Roberts 2007
Maps © Carl Rogers 2007
Photographs © Carl Rogers 2007

Photographs on pages 51, courtesy abraham photographic and 55, courtesy National
Library of Wales. Copyright.

Contents

Preface

N OT FAR TO GO NOW, you can see the summit looming ahead as you make your way up the last few hundred feet. Just below your path, the Snowdon train rattles past on its rack and pinion track to its halt just outside the summit 'hotel'. As the train disgorges it's passengers, you arrive, legs heavy as lead from that last few hundred feet of steep ground. However, you soon find that all the effort has been well worth it as your eyes fall upon the magnificent panorama that confronts you. From this, the highest point in all England and Wales, you can look right down into mid Wales, then along the curve of Cardigan Bay to the far end of Pembrokeshire. If you are lucky and the Irish sea is calm and clear, the Wicklow hills in Ireland can just be made out, while above you, floating effortlessly on the air currents, a Kestrel seeks it's prey, watching, waiting for that unsuspecting pipit or lark to appear.

Irrespective of how you have arrived, either by foot or by the train, the beauty of the scenery will soon charm and captivate you and having at last fulfilled your ambition to come up here, I bet it won't be long before you will want to visit the mountain again.

It was during the summer of 1977 that I first ventured into the mountains of Snowdonia, taking up residence in a Bed & Breakfast in the village of Llanberis. From that first day I fell in love with the whole area and as the following days progressed, I walked path after path until my feet and legs ached from using muscles which, until then, I didn't even know I had.

I knew that I had found a haven from the hustle and bustle of modern day life, if only a temporary one. I felt sorry for those who live, work and play in cities and never venture out into the hills and smell the fresh air of the countryside.

What I found, and I'm sure many others who come to Snowdonia on a regular basis have also found, is that the pace of life is slower here, you become master of your life once more, and not the slave.

Today, 30 years later, having climbed Snowdon over 100 times, not to mention many more of the surrounding peaks, I still have that same feeling every time I arrive in what has become at least my Shangri La.

In our modern high speed world that is changing daily, isn't it nice to know that here at least, time can stand still, if you are only prepared to stop awhile and enjoy it.

However, as I walk, my thoughts often dwell on the past—just imagine, these hills and mountains haven't changed at all in hundreds of years and probably very little since Roman soldiers marched through the Llanberis Pass 1,800 years ago. In fact, traces of a Roman road can still just be made out in the Pass, just as there are remains of a fort used by them on the pass near the Pen-y-Gwryd Hotel.

In many places there are traces left by people of the Stone, Bronze, and Iron Ages. During the 5th century there are thought to have been Irish settlements near the foot of Snowdon in Cwm Dyli, and in the 1850s the remains of a prehistoric canoe was found in Llyn Llydaw when the miners were building the causeway.

But the period that really interests me is much nearer to our own time. I often find myself thinking about the people who came to this area in the 19th century and the early years of the 20th century. What were their lives like in this hostile terrain as they struggled to hack a living from these hillsides?

I have put the results of my research into a short chapter at the end of the book and hope it will answer some of the questions raised by the many abandoned mines, quarries and associated ruins which you will see on your walks.

R. Russell Roberts, Wrexham, September 2002

An introduction to Snowdon

S NOWDON IS NOT ONLY the highest peak in the British Isles south of the Scottish Highlands, it is also the grandest. Yr Wyddfa, its highest point, heads a complex of ridges and subsidiary peaks separated by deep glacial valleys and dramatic rock scenery which has drawn climbers, mountaineers and walkers for over two centuries. But it is as the highest mountain in England and Wales that Snowdon is best known and is the main reason for attracting over half a million visitors per year, many of whom know little about the mountain until they are standing on its summit. So if you are reading this book before making an ascent, let us take a closer look at this superb mountain.

The name 'Snowdon' stands out amongst its neighbours, whose seemingly vowel-free spellings give visitors from across the border endless pronunciation problems. 'Snowdon' on the other hand, rolls off the English tongue with great ease. The name is of early Saxon origin meaning 'snowy hills' (from 'Snaudune'), and was originally applied not to one mountain, but to the whole range of high mountains which fall into the northern part of what is today called Snowdonia. It was only much later that the name came to be associated with the highest mountain in the group. But Snowdon's earliest name remains—Yr

Snowdon, Crib Goch and Crib y Ddysgl from the east

The classic view of Snowdon from Llynnau Mymbyr, Capel Curig

Wyddfa—the burial mound of the mythical giant Rhita Gawr who was said to have roamed these hills wearing a cloak made from the beards of the many kings who unsuccessfully challenged him. He is said to have finally met his end at the hands of none other than King Arthur. Ironically, Arthur is also said to have died on Snowdon on the pass known today as 'Bwlch-y-Saethau ('Pass of Arrows') from the fatal hail of arrows fired by his enemies.

It is fitting then that the name 'Snowdon' still refers, not to just one peak, but to a group of summits—a massif.

The complex layout of this massif is based on six main ridges which radiate to all points of the compass like the spokes of a wheel. These ridges are in turn separated by a series of deep valleys or cwms ('cwm' is the Welsh name for a high mountain 'bowl' or 'basin' shaped glacial valley). All of these cwms are long and deeply-cut by glacial action; even those to the south and west—the sides of Welsh mountains which are normally rounded, grassy and often featureless. On the north and east sides of the mountain, where glaciers were most active, the resulting landscape is almost Alpine. Cwm Dyli is the most impressive of all. At its head the summit buttress of Snowdon falls 480 metres (1,580 feet) to the blue-green waters of Glaslyn and will likely provide one of the most memorable images of the mountain for walkers on the Miners' Track. Lower down, the valley opens out into a vast amphitheatre hold-

Snowdon (Yr Wyddfa), Crib Goch and Crib y Ddysgl from Capel Curig

The rocky profile of Crib Goch from the east

ing the 2km-long Llyn Llydaw. The power of the ice is demonstrated by the depth of these lakes; Glaslyn's rock floor plunges to 127 feet (38 metres) and Llydaw's to an incredible 190 feet (58 metres).

Also demonstrating the power of moving ice is the unspoilt Cwm Glas. This is a classic example of a 'hanging valley', perched high above the Llanberis Pass, with two small jewel-like pools reflecting the dark crags which surround it. There is just one infrequently used route which passes through the cwm, so it is often one of the quietest parts of the mountain.

Another impressive valley is Cwm Llan immediately south of the main summit. It is probably the deepest-cut of all the valleys with Yr Wyddfa towering 700 metres (2,200 feet) above the valley floor. Cwm Clogwyn to the west and Cwm Brwynog to the north-west also have a classic glacial form with steep cliff-lined headwalls and small lakes, but they are less deeply-cut.

The ridges which separate these cwms radiate out from two high summits—Yr Wyddfa and Garnedd Ugain, better known as Crib y Ddysgl. They are separated by a connecting ridge just 1km long and

Snowdon and the huge precipice of Clogwyn Du'r Arddu

only just dipping below 1,000 metres briefly at Bwlch Glas (998m). The shortest of the ridges falls to the north-west and is just 2km long while the longest is over 5km, reaching from the summit of Crib y Ddysgl at 1,065 metres down to the medieval ruins of Castell Dolbadarn on the shores of Llyn Padarn at just 120 metres above sea level.

All Snowdon's ridges are lined by cliffs on at least one side (usually the north or east) and two of the highest precipices in Wales are to be found here—Clogwyn Du'r Arddu, which can be seen impressively from the Llanberis Path, and the northern cliffs of Y Lliwedd, which form the southern wall of the great amphitheatre of Cwm Dyli.

But the grandest ridge of all is the narrow edge separating Cwm Dyli from Cwm Glas and the Llanberis Pass. Sharpened to a knife edge by glacial action on both sides, this ridge is a classic 'arête', a term usually reserved for Alpine ridges. A traverse of the ridge is the most challenging and exhilarating ascent, not just of Snowdon, but of any mountain south of the Scottish Highlands. The most sensational section is over Crib Goch where a narrow rock ridge connects the eastern summit with the famous 'Pinnacles'. A steady foot and a head for heights is called for, but under fine summer conditions it should be within the capabilities of anyone prepared to do some scrambling.

Across the void of Cwm Dyli stands the smooth 300 metre face of Y Lliwedd, legendary resting place of King Arthur and his knights. Though not as narrow and sensational as Crib Goch, a traverse of this peak, along with its connecting ridge via Bwlch-y-Saethau, forms the southern arm of the Snowdon Horseshoe, a route which provides one the finest mountain days in Britain.

A number of minor ridges on the northern flanks of the mountain provide even harder Alpine type scrambles and easy rock climbs but are beyond the scope of this guide.

The other ridge of note is the South Ridge which forms the western arm of Cwm Llan. This rises from Bwlch Cwm Llan and narrows considerably at the famous Bwlch Main, although it nowhere approaches the severity of Crib Goch.

For the walker there is an almost bewildering choice of paths on every side of the mountain—probably more routes of ascent than any other peak in Britain. There are six main paths—sometimes referred to as the 'Classic Paths'—two on the western ridges; one from the south; one from the north and two which ascend from the east by the

The narrow crest of Crib Goch which separates Cwm Dyli and Cwm Glas

Snowdon summit and the South Ridge from the west

dramatic Cwm Dyli. These are all well established routes which have been in use for at least a century and some for much longer. They are well used trails and under normal conditions following them should not be a problem. They are all well served with car parks, although their popularity can cause congestion (both on the mountain and in the car parks and adjacent roads) on occasions at peak times in the summer. These paths are described in the first section of the book.

In addition to the 'Classic Paths' there are a number of less well known paths. Some of these are variations on the 'Classic Paths', such as the South Ridge which provides a variation on the Watkin or Rhyd Ddu Paths. Others, such as Crib Goch and Y Lliwedd, are more difficult and require scrambling which, during the 19th century, would have been regarded as climbs and were thus avoided by the vast majority. These routes are described in the second section.

As well as the high tops of the mountain there are a few minor summits which, although part of the Snowdon massif, are overlooked by the vast majority because none of the usual routes pass their way and the vast height difference of their near neighbour makes them appear insignificant. The most shapely of these is Yr Aran which forms one of the enclosing arms of Cwm Llan and is seen to perfection from Llyn Gwynant. If this lovely little mountain stood alone it would be one of Snowdonia's most famous peaks.

Also suffering from the proximity of their giant neighbour is the group of hills which terminate in the rounded bulk of Moel Eilio. This is really an extension of Snowdon's short north-west ridge but Bwlch Cwm Brwynog cuts so deeply that the group appears to stand alone. The third section of the book deals with these outlying hills (routes 12-14).

Finally, mention should be made of the equipment necessary to explore the mountain safely. The vast numbers who ascend Snowdon— many with little or no experience of the mountains—have inevitably resulted in accidents. The majority have occurred in winter when, under harsh icy conditions, nearly all the routes become 'Alpine' and will require high performance clothing, an ice axe and preferably crampons. If you have little or no experience of winter mountain walking or the equipment required, stay off the mountain in these conditions.

This book has been written with the summer visitor in mind and in dry conditions with good visibility all the 'Classic Paths' will be easy to follow. Equipment can thus be minimal although you should be prepared to spend five to seven hours on the mountain. Enough food

The shapely summit of Yr Aran from the Rhyd Ddu approach

and liquids should always be carried because, although the summit cafe offers refreshments in the summer months, you will need food and liquids throughout the ascent and descent.

You should also be prepared for a change in the weather and lower temperatures as you near the summit. The temperature can drop by as much as 10 degrees Centigrade between the valley and the summit. Also, in very hot or clear conditions you will need protection from the sun (yes, even in Wales!).

Due to the rough, rocky terrain, good walking boots are the only footwear to be recommended even on the finest summer day, although many ascend the mountain in training shoes. If you follow their example be prepared for twisted ankles along with knocks and injuries from rocks on the scree slopes which you will encounter on all the routes. Training shoes and other light footwear should never be used if there is any likelihood of encountering snow and ice on the mountain.

The 'Classic Paths' are purely footpaths and even the steepest sections require no scrambling. Routes 7–11 however, will require at least some use of the hands. The South Ridge narrows for a short section where scrambling may be required here and there. Similarly with the path over Y Lliwedd, although the route is mainly walking. Crib Goch on the other hand, is completely different. The scrambling is sustained and the positions exposed, and although nowhere is it technically hard, you will need to be able to cope with the exposure. If this is not you, avoid the route.

The Six 'Classic Paths'

1. Llanberis Path
2. Pyg Track
3. Miners' Track
4. Watkin Path
5. Rhyd Ddu Path
6. Snowdon Ranger Path

LLANBERIS
YHA

Llyn Peris

Park and Ride

Nant Peris

Snowdon Mountain Railway

1

Moel Eilio

Llyn Dwythwch

Halfway Station

Bwlch Maesgwyn

Welsh Highland Railway

A4085

Foel Goch

Moel Cynghorion

Bwlch Brwynog

Llyn Du'r Arddu

Clogwyn Station

Snowdon Ranger

YHA

6

Llyn Ffynnon y-gwas

Cwm Clogwyn

Llyn Cwellyn

SNOWDON
YR WYDDFA

Rhyd-Ddu

South Ridge

Cwm Llan

5

Llyn y Gader

Bwlch Cwm Llan

Yr Aran

BEDDGELERT

A map of Snowdon showing routes 1-6

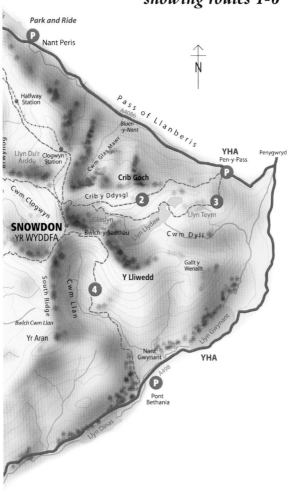

1. Llanberis Path

Distance/time: *7.25km (4½ miles)/3-4hrs*

Height gained: *990m (3,270ft)*

Outline: *This is the easiest and longest way up Snowdon and is therefore the most popular of the six usual routes. For most of the way it follows the track of the Snowdon Mountain Railway from Llanberis on what is a gentle graded and well used footpath.*

Start: *There is plenty of parking space opposite the Snowdon Mountain Railway in Llanberis, but during the high season the car parks get very crowded, so you need to get there fairly early. Grid ref: 582 589.*

Ascent: From the station walk right (left from car park) along the road and take the first turning on the right immediately opposite the 'Royal Victoria Hotel' ('Victoria Terrace'). At the end of the road, cross the cattle grid and begin the long climb up a steep road with the railway on your right (about 1km).

At the top of this road go through the gate by 'Pen Ceunant Uchaf' on the right and about 200m further on, turn left onto the signed footpath.

The path now goes on gently with a steady rise, dipping under the railway in about 2km, then after a fairly level stretch you will reach the newly refurbished 'Halfway House' where you can buy refreshments. After the 'Halfway House', the path becomes harder and steeper. On your right the ground falls away into Cwm Brwynog, to the cold dark waters of Llyn Du'r Arddu reflecting the even darker wall of Clogwyn Du'r Arddu, a popular climbing ground for the serious rock climber.

As you follow the path past Cwm Brwynog fork left where the path splits (the path ahead is used by rock climbers to reach Clogwyn Du'r Arddu) and rise to go under the railway track again near the Clogwyn Station (see photo opposite). Here you will find yourself looking down into Cwm Glas Bach (sometimes known as 'Cwm Hetiau' meaning 'Cwm of the hats' from the numerous hats blow from passengers on the train), the Llanberis Pass and across to the Glyder ridge.

The path now swings across the broad back of Crib y Ddysgl with the railway below to the right. Don't be tempted to follow the railway here as there are steep cliffs immediately below. Meet the railway again just before Bwlch Glas where there is a 2m upright stone and stunning views down into Cwm Dyli to Glaslyn and Llyn Llydaw.

From here you have a steady walk up to the summit and no doubt, a well earned drink in the Café.

Aerial view of the upper section of the Llaberis Path and the Snowdon Mountain Railway

2. Pyg Track

Distance/time: *5.25km (3¼ miles)/3hrs*

Height gained: *795m (2,605ft)*

Outline: *A gradual climb along a rocky but well constructed path leads to Bwlch Moch. From here you enter the Snowdon Horseshoe with its grand scenery. Old mine workings add extra interest in the approach to Cwm Glaslyn, before the final climb up the famous 'Zig Zags' to the ridge to join the Snowdon Mountain Railway and the Llanberis Path, which is followed to the summit.*

Start: *There is a moderate sized car park at Pen-y-Pass. A fee is payable. Grid ref: 647 557. If this is full (likely in the summer) use the Park and Ride situated in Nant Peris. Grid ref: 606 583.*

Ascent: The obvious exit from the lower car park is the Miners' Track, the Pyg Track exits from the higher car park just behind the cafe ('Gorphwysfa Restaurant') through a gap in the stone wall and under power lines. A well constructed path—with views down the Llanberis Pass—leads to Bwlch Moch, the point at which you enter the Snowdon Horseshoe. From here there are views down to Llyn Llydaw and it's causeway, and beyond to the 300m face of Y Lliwedd. Ahead is Snowdon, looking deceptively close.

On the Pyg Track approaching Snowdon

To the right here is the steep path leading up to Crib Goch, but the Pyg Track continues over the stiles ahead to contour along the mountain's southern slopes.

Following the path you eventually reach a superb viewpoint where Glaslyn and the dramatic summit cone of Snowdon can be seen to perfection rising almost 500m above the lake.

Continue on the contouring path to an even closer viewpoint directly above Glaslyn. From here the path curves around the cwm past the junction with the Miners' Track coming up from the left and the remains of the copper mines. Higher up you reach the foot of the famous 'Zig Zags' which negotiate the final steep slopes to the stone pillar on the bwlch which indicates the junction with the Llanberis Path and the Snowdon Mountain Railway. Turn left for the final ten minute walk to the summit.

3. Miners' Track

Distance/time: *7km (4¼ miles)/3hrs*

Height gained: *795m (2,605ft)*

Outline: *A path which rises at a gentle gradient until you reach Llyn Llydaw, then a steep climb brings you to Glaslyn directly below Snowdon itself. Above Glaslyn, steep, loose scree leads to a junction with the Pyg Track and then the famous 'Zig Zags'. The final section follows the Snowdon Mountain Railway and the Llanberis Path.*

Start: *As for route 2. Grid ref: 647 557.*

Ascent: The Miners' Track leaves the lower car park by the obvious exit opposite the entrance and begins as a gentle, rough, road-like track originally built to transport ore from the mines high up on the mountain. Follow the track with views left to Moel Siabod and down to the vale of Gwynant. Soon the track contours right to pass above Llyn Teyrn and the remains of barracks used to house miners.

At Llyn Llydaw you are in the centre of the famous Snowdon Horseshoe with the dramatic cliffs of Y Lliwedd to the left, Crib Goch to the right and Snowdon directly ahead.

Cross the causeway (built in 1853 to serve the upper mines), and follow the path as it winds left along the far shore passing the derelict mine built in 1898 by the Britannia Copper Mine Ltd and closed during the First World War in 1916. Having passed these buildings the going starts to get tougher as the path rises fairly steeply to the basin-like cwm holding Glaslyn ('green lake') where you will get superb views of the north-east face of Snowdon rising steeply above the grey-green water.

Follow the path right around the northern shore of Glaslyn, and after derelict buildings on the right, turn right to start a steep climb to join the Pyg Track. Turn left to reach the famous 'Zig Zags' (in winter conditions this section of the route can be very hazardous).

The 'Zig Zags' lead up to a large 2-metre stone (photo below) on the skyline (a useful marker in mist) which marks the end of the path. Here you join the Llanberis Path and the Snowdon Mountain Railway which you now follow left to the summit.

Snowdon from Bwlch Glas where the Pyg Track, Miners' Track and Llanberis Path meet

4. *Watkin Path*

Distance/time: *7km (4¼ miles)/4hrs*

Height gained: *1,086m (3,560ft)*

Outline: *This path is possibly the most arduous of the six main routes up Snowdon and involves the most height gain. To compensate, it is possibly the most beautiful, beginning in the woods of Nantgwynant and rising beside the cascading river into Cwm Llan with its old mine workings and dramatic scenery. Steeper walking then takes you up onto the high shoulder of the mountain followed by the final very steep upper slopes.*

Start: *Pont Bethania car park near Nantgwynant on the A498 road to Beddgelert. Grid Ref: 628 507.*

Ascent: Turn left out of the car park, cross the bridge and in about 100m or so turn right into a narrow lane. Don't follow the lane, instead go up stone steps immediately ahead, signed for the Watkin Path. This new section of path weaves through mature woods above the old lane to eventually join a rough track with a view out over the valley. Go left through the gate (signed 'Watkin') and follow the rising track, soon with the cascading Afon Cwm Llan down to your right.

Ignore a path on the right which drops to a stone footbridge over the stream immediately before a gate and above a large waterfall, continuing ahead on the well made path ahead into Cwm Llan. The path levels abruptly as you enter the cwm and a left fork goes off immediately to gain the South Ridge. Ignore this path continuing ahead to cross the river, passing the ruined farmhouse of Plas Cwm Llan and curving left past the Gladstone Rock.

As a point of interest, Plas Cwm Llan, was used during World War II by Commando's rehearsing for the D-Day landings. Near the Gladstone Rock is a plaque commemorating Mr Gladstone's visit to Wales in September 1892 when he addressed the local people standing on top of this rock. He was 84 years old at the time.

Walk on, soon passing through the spoil heaps of the South Snowdon Slate Quarry on a surfaced path, bearing right beyond ruins which are all that remain of the barracks and dressing sheds used by the quarry men during the week (just like the ones at Llyn Teyrn on the Miners' Track). They would make their way home at the weekend for a few hours before having to return, ready for Monday morning and another week of back breaking labour.

A clear path lies ahead of you until you reach Bwlch Ciliau ('pass of the retreat') on the edge of the cliffs overlooking Cwm Dyli. Go over to the edge of the cliffs for a wonderful view into Cwm Dyli with it's dramatic scenery.

Turn left on a contouring path (photo below) to Bwlch-y-Saethau ('Pass of Arrows') where according to Welsh tradition King Arthur was killed by a flight of arrows fired by his defeated enemies as they fled towards Cwm Dyli. There is a dramatic view down to Glaslyn and across to the famous Zig Zags from here.

You are now faced with a rough steep ascent over loose scree. The path is badly eroded in parts and the angle of the climb is quite steep. The path cuts diagonally across the slope from right to left to reach a 2-metre marker stone indicating the junction with the Rhyd Ddu Path on the South Ridge. Turn right up the ridge to the summit.

Approaching Snowdon on the Watkin Path just below Bwlch-y-Saethau

5. Rhyd Ddu Path

Distance/time: *6km (3¾ miles)/3-4hrs*

Height gained: *900m (2,975ft)*

Outline: *This path approaches Snowdon by the more gentle but featureless south-western slopes of the mountain. Interest develops as height is gained and a circle is made of the dramatic headwall of Cwm Clogwyn above the precipice of Llechog. The narrow South Ridge is joined for the final climb to the summit.*

Start: *Pay and display car park immediately south of the village of Rhyd Ddu on the A4085. Grid ref: 571 526.*

Ascent: Walk north past the WC block for 100m or so and turn right through a gate to cross the Welsh Highland Railway by a level crossing. Follow a rough farm road (signed to 'Fridd Isaf') which rises gently through the lower pastures passing a deep quarry pit.

In about 1.5km and shortly after a ladder stile, turn left off the track through a kissing gate (the track ahead continues to Bwlch Cwm Llan at the foot of the South Ridge – route 10) and onto a narrower path through rocky and sometimes boggy ground.

Snowdon from the west showing the upper section of the Rhyd Ddu Path

Bwlch Main on the South Ridge

Go through a gap in a low crumbling wall which runs diagonally across the path, then a second gap much higher up. A roofless ruin here was a halfway house many years ago where an old lady and her son made refreshments for walkers.

After a third dry stone wall, the path curves out onto the rounded shoulder of Llechog and you pass through the wall again on the edge of Cwm Clogwyn. The path now follows the edge of the cliffs with views down into Cwm Clogwyn and ahead to Snowdon rising above the broken headwall of the cwm.

At the eastern end of the ridge the path zig zags up to join the South Ridge. Bear left to cross Bwlch Main, sometimes known as 'The Saddle' where the ridge narrows considerably to give dramatic views into both Cwm Tregalan and Cwm Clogwyn. Keep to the right-hand side of the ridge initially before returning to the left-hand side for the final climb to the summit passing the upright stone which marks the exit of the Watkin Path.

6. Snowdon Ranger Path

Distance/time: *6.25km (4 miles)/3-4hrs*

Height gained: *954m (3,130ft)*

Outline: *This is one of the easier paths up the mountain and is also believed to be the oldest, being named after John Morton who called himself the 'Snowdon Ranger' and used to guide Victorian gentlemen to the summit.*

The early stages of the walk can be wet as you will cover boggy ground, before a rise is made close to, but out of sight of the huge cliffs of Clogwyn Du'r Arddu. The final section is shared with the Llanberis Path and the Snowdon Mountain Railway.

Start: *There is a car park opposite the Snowdon Ranger Youth Hostel on the A4085. Grid Ref: 565 551.*

Ascent: Cross the road and take the signed footpath and bridleway almost opposite beside the driveway to 'Caer Orsaf'. Cross the track of the Welsh Highland Railway turning left and then right up the track to 'Llwyn Onn farm'. Above the farm the path zig zags up the hillside gaining height quickly.

The upper section of the Snowdon Ranger Path

The lower section of the Snowdon Ranger Path

After a gate in a wall the angle eases and the path crosses flatter more boggy ground. The ridge can be seen rising ahead and there are good views into Cwm Clogwyn to the right.

The path rises almost to the bwlch on the left and above the waters of Llyn Ffynnon-y-Gwas. A short diversion to your left gives a fine view into Cwm Brwynog and in the distance the Llanberis Path. From here the path begins to zig zag up onto the ridge above. This is the toughest section of the climb but it is soon over. Higher up, the ridge narrows as you approach the top of the cliffs of Clogwyn Du'r Arddu.

If you have a good head for heights turn to your left a little and have a good look at this awesome 200m precipice where some of the hardest rock climbs in North Wales have been pioneered.

Returning to the path, continue the climb until the angle eases and the path widens into a broad stony plateau. The going now becomes much easier and soon you swing right to cross the Snowdon Mountain Railway and join the Llanberis Path at the 2-metre upright stone on Bwlch Glas with its stunning views into Cwm Dyli. From here it is about another ten minutes or so to the summit up to the right.

Other Routes

A map of Snowdon showing routes 7-14

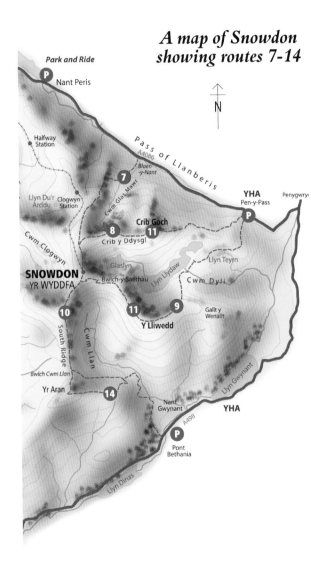

7. Gyrn Las Ridge

Distance/time: *4km (2½ miles)/3hrs*

Height gained: *1,000m (3,280ft)*

Outline: *This route will be favoured by those who enjoy solitude. The wild rugged beauty of Cwm Glas and Cwm Glas Mawr is seen to perfection from an easy though interesting ridge with short sections of scrambling. The setting is magnificent and as the route is relatively unknown you are likely to avoid the crowds. It is not recommended in poor visibility or as a descent without prior knowledge of the route.*

Start: Blaen-y-Nant in the Llanberis Pass on the A4086 (grid ref: 623 570). Parking could be a problem. If the laybys are full (likely during the summer) park at Nant Peris and take the Park and Ride.

Ascent: Cross the bridge at Blaen-y-Nant, go over the stile ahead and cross another wooden bridge on the right. Here you turn sharp left to follow the right bank of the stream.

Follow the path (which is not very clear due to little use except by the occasional rock climber) until you reach a wall. Pass through the gap in this wall and you will see a much clearer path ahead of you. This leads up into Cwm Glas Mawr.

The Gyrn Las Ridge from Blaean-y-Nant

Looking into Cwm Glas to Crib Goch from the top of the Gyrn Las Ridge

As you enter the cwm the angle eases and there are two large boulders which the path passes between. Bear right at this point up the grassy slopes to gain the ridge. A faint path will be seen here and there, but once on the ridge a visible path has become established. The lower part of the ridge is a straightforward walk but as you gain height you begin to use your hands more and more.

The setting is magnificent with superb views into the gulf of Cwm Glas Mawr and Cwm Glas Bach, although no where is the exposure on the scale of Crib Goch.

The upper section of the ridge has two easy sections of scrambling with little or no exposure, before you find yourself on the broad grassy shoulder of Crib y Ddysgl looking across Cwm Glas to the fantastic rock architecture of Crib Goch's pinnacles (photo above) and the imposing nose of Clogwyn-y-Person (supposedly named after a 19th century parson who loved walking the ridges, and who is widely believed to have made hill walking and scrambling the popular sport it is today).

From here you can either join the Llanberis Route which you will see away to the right, or continue along the rim of the cwm to Crib y Ddysgl and then on to Snowdon.

8. Crib Goch

Distance/time: *5.25km (3¼ miles)/3-4hrs*

Height gained: *895m (2,940ft)*

Outline: *This is the most challenging route up Snowdon and is justifiably popular. In normal conditions it provides an enjoyable exhilarating scramble with fine situations, but in poor weather or winter conditions, it becomes a climb and should be treated as such.*

The route traverses the 1.5km ridge of Crib Goch and Crib y Ddysgl and forms half of the classic Snowdon Horseshoe. An exciting scramble to Crib Goch's superb rock summit is followed by exposed scrambling along a narrow rock ridge to the famous 'Pinnacles'. The rise to Crib y Ddysgl contains more scrambling but of an easier standard. Beyond Crib y Ddysgl the Llanberis Path is followed to the summit.

Start: *As for route 2. Grid Ref: 647 557.*

Ascent: From the car park follow the Pyg Track (route 2) to Bwlch-y-Moch.

Traversing the Crib Goch Pinnacles with Snowdon and Crib y Ddysgl behind

Here the path forks. The Pyg Track continues over stiles ahead to contour the southern slopes of Crib Goch, whilst the Crib Goch path bears right up over the shoulder. The path has been surfaced with large stone slabs making it almost impossible to miss. Higher up your way is barred by the large rock step guarding the east ridge.

The left-hand side of this step is both steep and hard while the right-hand side eventually merges into the east face. The most frequented line is almost direct and involves moderate rock scrambling up a series of grooves and corners. Once above the rock step the easier rocks of the upper east ridge lead spectacularly to the summit.

This is the most dramatic summit in Snowdonia and if you can relax it is a good place to rest and enjoy the fantastic scenery that surrounds you. The knife edge of the north ridge sweeps down into the Llanberis Pass, but it is likely to be the narrow ridge ahead which will grab your attention. The views are magnificent.

The ridge is narrow, almost level and exposed for about 300m (see photo opposite). If you are at all doubtful on this section drop down a few feet on the left side which will give you a little protection from the exposure on the north side, but not too far.

The ridge eventually leads to the first of the rocky 'Pinnacles' from where you will get a wonderful view down into Cwm Uchaf ('Higher Cwm') below on your right.

The 'Pinnacles' can be tackled direct or turned on the left but be careful not to descend too far. The final pinnacle has an optional short exposed section on the north side (right) overlooking a gully and requiring care, but once over this section the descent to the grass col of Bwlch Coch is easy. The major difficulties are now over.

The ridge is now much wider, far less exposed and rises to one last rock step on the approach to Crib y Ddysg. There is a short narrow section before the summit which can be turned on the right.

From Crib y Ddysgl make the easy gentle descent to Bwlch Glas where you join the Llanberis Path and the routes coming up the 'Zig Zags' from Glaslyn. A short moderate walk of about ten minutes will take you to the summit.

9. Y Lliwedd

Distance/time: *7km (4¼ miles)/4hrs*

Height gained: *1,010m (3,320ft)*

Outline: *This walk is usually completed in reverse as the second half of the Snowdon Horseshoe. Although the scenery is equally grand, there is little scrambling making it a much easier option than Crib Goch.*

Start: *As for route 2. Grid Ref: 647 557.*

Ascent: Follow the Miners' Track (route 3) to Llyn Llydaw. As you approach the shore of the lake turn left at an obvious fork near the pumping house. The path follows the shore at first then rises quite steeply to the col between Gallt-y-Wenallt on your left and Y Lliwedd Bach on your right.

A prominent cairn marks entry onto the ridge (a useful marker in misty conditions). Turn right and keep along the crest of the ridge.

Y Lliwedd and Cwm Dyli from Bwlch Glas

Looking towards Snowdon from Y Lliwedd

There are sensational views on your right into Cwm Dyli to Llyn Llydaw over 400m below and ahead to Snowdon.

There is a slight drop to a col beyond the shoulder of the mountain, then a steep rise to the twin summits (highest point is the west peak) of Y Lliwedd.

From the summit continue along the edge of the cliffs making the descent to Bwlch Ciliau ('pass of the retreat') where the Watkin Path joins from Cwm Llan on the left. Continue to Bwlch-y-Saethau ('Pass of Arrows').

You are now faced with a rough steep ascent to the summit shared with the upper section of the Watkin Path. The slope is composed of loose scree which is badly eroded and the angle of the climb is quite steep. The path cuts diagonally across the slope from right to left to reach the 2-metre upright stone indicating the junction with the Rhyd-Ddu Path on the South Ridge. You are now only five minutes from the summit up to the right.

10. South Ridge

Distance/time: *7km (4¼ miles)/4hrs*

Height gained: *1,100m (3,660ft)*

Outline: *This route offers an alternative ascent or descent from the starting points of either the Watkin Path or the Rhyd Ddu Path and uses the fine South Ridge of the mountain for the upper section.*

The walking is easy in the lower sections following well constructed paths. The upper section of the South Ridge has a short narrow section involving an easy scramble with a little exposure.

Start: *As for the Watkin Path (route 4) – grid Ref: 627 506, or the Rhyd Ddu Path (route 5) – grid ref: 571 526.*

Ascent: Follow the Watkin Path (route 4) into Cwm Llan.

Immediately on entering the Cwm and before crossing the stream, bear left and follow a steep diagonal footpath to the course of the old tramway. Turn right along the tramway and follow it almost to its end adjacent to spoil heaps over to the right. From here a path on the left

Looking down the South Ridge from the summit of Snowdon

Descending the South Ridge towards Yr Aran

heads directly up to reach Bwlch Cwm Llan at the base of the South Ridge with Yr Aran to the left.

(Alternatively, start from Rhyd Ddu. Walk north past the WC block for 100m or so and turn right through a gate to cross the Welsh Highland Railway by a level crossing. Follow a rough farm road (signed to 'Fridd Isaf') which rises gently through the lower pastures passing a deep quarry pit. In about 1.5km and shortly after a ladder stile, the Rhyd Ddu Path goes left off the track through a kissing gate. Ignore this, continuing on the track ahead to Bwlch Cwm Llan at the foot of the South Ridge.)

Turn right up recently built stone steps (or left if approaching from Rhyd Ddu) and ascend the ridge near its crest to a subsidiary summit at 931m. The next section narrows at its junction with the Rhyd Ddu Path and there is a dip to Bwlch Main ('narrow pass'). Continue on the right-hand side of the ridge at first then on the left-hand side to reach the summit.

11. Snowdon Horseshoe

Distance/time: *11.5km (7¼ miles)/6-9hrs*

Height gained: *1,200m (3,940ft)*

Outline: *The Snowdon Horseshoe offers a magnificent mountain day which can not be rivalled by anything south of the Scottish Highlands. It follows the skyline of Cwm Dyli formed by the two great eastern ridges of Y Lliwedd and Crib Goch. The route provides moderate, exposed scrambling for much of its length. Crib Goch provides the hardest section with the return leg over Y Lliwedd offering grand views from the top of the largest precipice in Wales. This section involves rough, rocky walking rather than the type of scrambling encountered on Crib Goch.*

Start: *As for route 2. Grid ref: 647 557.*

Ascent: Follow the directions for route 8 over Crib Goch and Crib y Ddysgl to the summit of Snowdon. From here descend the upper section of the Watkin Path leaving the South Ridge at the upright stone and crossing the south face of the mountain diagonally to Bwlch-y-Saethau.

Crib Goch from Bwlch-y-Saethau

Looking across Cwm Dyli from Crib y Ddysgl to Y Lliwedd during a perfect cloud inversion

Y Lliwedd from Bwlch-y-Saethau

(Here you can cut the route short if needed by scrambling down the ridge—Y Gribin—which drops to Glaslyn, but don't attempt it unless you were completely happy on Crib Goch. The standard is similar. Keep to the left of the crest away from the huge drop into Cwm Dyli. In poor visibility it would be hard to locate the start of the ridge and should not be attempted without prior knowledge of the route.)

From Bwlch-y-Saethau follow the Watkin Path down to Bwlch Ciliau where it turns right down into Cwm Llan. Keep ahead here on the path which follows the edge of the cliffs to Y Lliwedd which can be seen rising ahead (photo above).

Traverse the twin summits of Y Lliwedd and follow the good path down to a cairn marking the exit from the ridge. From here drop down to the outflow of Llyn Llydaw to join the Miners' Track and return to Pen-y-Pass.

Outlying Peaks

12. Moel Eilio

Distance/time: *12km (7½ miles)/3-4hrs (including return)*

Height gained: *790m (2,600ft)*

Outline: *This mountain group suffers from the proximity of its larger and more famous neighbour. As a result it is overlooked by the majority who only have eyes for Snowdon. However, it provides an excellent ridge walk with superb views, particularly of Snowdon and is often clear when the higher peaks wear a cap of cloud.*

Start: *There are a number of car parks in Llanberis. Begin the walk in 'Ffordd Capel Coch' (Capel Coch Road). This is the road signed for the Youth Hostel from the main street. Grid Ref: 578 601.*

Ascent: From the centre of Llanberis follow the road 'Ffordd Capel Coch'. Pass the Youth Hostel on the left in about 600m and carry on past the farmhouse called 'Hafod Lydan'. Where the road turns left immediately after the house 'Hafod Uchaf' on the left (about 1km from Llanberis), turn right along a track. Go through the gate or over the stile and continue until you are about 50m from the wall and stile ahead. Turn left onto a path which rises to a gate and stile in the wall.

Looking back along the ridge to Moel Eilio

The view south from Moel Eilio to Llyn Cwellyn and the Eifionydd hills

Go through the gate and continue along the path until the lake comes into view. Turn right up steep grass (no path) to the crest of the ridge. Once on the rounded crest of the ridge turn left and walk beside the fence. There are faint footpaths on both sides of the fence and stiles over any crossing fences. Near the summit join the broad path which rises up the flat northern flanks of the mountain. The summit at 726m (2,380ft) is marked by a circular drystone shelter.

The ridge continues south-east to Bwlch Cwm Cesig with Cwm Dwythwch and Llyn Dwythwch down below to your left. From the bwlch climb to Foel Gron (593m) and Foel Goch beyond at 605m.

The return to Llanberis can be made either by the broad grass ridge leading north from Foel Goch, or a steep grassy descent south-east which will bring you down to the col between Foel Goch and Moel Cynghorion (Bwlch Maesgwm). Turn left onto the path (thought to be an ancient packhorse trail) passing the farmhouse of 'Brithdir' and continuing along the track to 'Ffordd Capel Coch'. Follow this lane back to Llanberis.

13. Moel Cynghorion

Distance/time: *8km (5 miles)/3hrs (including return)*

Height gained: *565m (1,850ft)*

Outline: *This hill separates the Moel Eilio group from Snowdon and provides an excellent viewpoint.*

An easy grassy ascent suitable for a half-day walk or as an alternative to the higher tops in poor weather.

Start: *As for the Snowdon Ranger Path (route 6).*
Grid Ref: 565 551.

Ascent: Follow route 6 to Bwlch Cwm Brwynog above Llyn Ffynnon-y-Gwas. Stay on the main path until you are just above the bwlch and directly above the lake where a narrower path turns left towards the fence. Follow the path by the fence across the bwlch and up the south-east ridge of the mountain with superb views of Clogwyn Du'r Arddu.

Descend the long easy angled west ridge to Bwlch Maesgwm. Take the path to the left to join the Snowdon Ranger Path to return.

Moel Cynghorion and Moel Eilio from Clogwyn Du'r Arddu

Yr Aran from Llyn Gwynant

14. Yr Aran

Distance/time: *9km (5¾ miles)/3hrs (including return)*

Height gained: *823m (2,700ft)*

Outline: *An interesting walk to one of Snowdonia's most shapely peaks and a fine viewpoint. It can be approached from both Cwm Llan (the Watkin Path) and Rhyd Ddu.*

Start: *As for the Watkin Path (route 4). Grid Ref: 628 506.*

Ascent: Follow the Watkin Path into Cwm Llan.

As soon as you reach level ground and about 100m before you cross the stream, turn left onto a path which rises to the old tramway which you cross.

The path soon swings left then curves right to wind its way over grass and later scree. Keep to the right of mine workings taking care near unfenced shafts. Pass a second mine and continue up grass to

Yr Aran framed by the woods of the Beddgelert Forest

the rounded ridge crest. Turn right along the ridge beside a wall. Where the wall turns right high up on the shoulder of the mountain, cross it by a stile and continue on to the summit.

Return either by the same route or by descending to Bwlch Cwm Llan at the foot of Snowdon's South Ridge (see the following paragraph) then turning right on the path into Cwm Llan to return by the Watkin Path.

An easier option is to follow the Watkin Path into Cwm Llan as before, but instead of crossing the old tramway, turn right along it and follow it almost to its end adjacent to spoil heaps over to the right. From here a path on the left heads directly up to reach Bwlch Cwm Llan at the base of the South Ridge of Snowdon with Yr Aran to the left. This point can also be reached from Rhyd Ddu—see the alternative start for route 10.

Turn left and soon a faint appears. Follow this up beside the wall on the right which swings left below the final rocks to join the east ridge. Go right to the summit.

Victorian mountaineers near the summit of Snowdon
© abraham photographic

Snowdon during the nineteenth century

Snowdon during the nineteenth century

'M sure that as you have followed some of the paths described in this book you have glanced at the many derelict buildings that abound and wondered to yourself "What went on in there?" or "What was that used for?" Well, now that you are back at home, or perhaps in your hotel or holiday cottage enjoying a good rest, you might enjoy a short trip into the industrial history of the mountain.

Unlike our great-grand parents who visited Snowdon in the 19th century, our ramblings among the mountains today are not interrupted by the work of miners drawing copper or lead out of the hillsides. When we puff and pant up the Zig Zags to Bwlch Glas carrying our modern light weight rucksacks and wearing our high performance clothing we don't have to step aside to let the miners pass as they carry heavy sacks of ore on their backs, so it can be taken on horse drawn sledges down to the shores of Llyn Cwellyn, to be transported to Caernarfon Docks.

As you walk along the Miners' Track past the remains of miner's barracks on the shore of Llyn Teyrn, the ruins stand quiet and empty, but during the second half of the 19th century miners would live there during the week only returning to their families at weekends. Imagine

The Britannia Copper Mine beside Llyn Llydaw

these men sitting outside on a warm evening after a long and tiring day smoking their clay pipes while discussing the events of the day. The tobacco, at 1½d per ounce (less than 1 pence per 28 grams), would be one of the few luxuries they could afford. If the weather was bad (as it frequently is on Snowdon) each man, or possibly two or three might huddle around the peat fire—on which no doubt a can of tea would be brewing—in the gloomy light of a candle which would throw weird shadows onto the walls and soot-blackened ceilings. These candles had to be bought by the men themselves at a cost of 3d (2p) per pound (0.5kg). Candles were bought by weight rather than quantity.

These one room 'cottages' were built in 1840, and another set were built higher up by Glaslyn 33 years later. Remember how bleak the weather can be in both summer and winter, and it gives you a good idea of what life for those hard working men was like. In fact most of the men only lived into their 40s (the average working week in England and Wales in 1882 was 78 hours, though many people worked much longer).

The beautiful silence that we take for granted now as we walk Snowdon's paths didn't exist a century or more ago, as the constant sound of the grinding mills by Llyn Llydaw and the water wheel which stood just where the stream came out of Glaslyn would have echoed through the cwm. There would also be the sound of blasting coming from inside the mountain as the miners created more levels (there were eight levels altogether) and tunnelled far into the mountainside. If you glance at the western shore of Glaslyn you will see a small ruined building set apart from everything else—this was the Gunpowder Store.

Did the Victorians have a cafe where they could stop and have a cuppa on the way to the summit I hear you ask? Well, actually they did, for just by Glaslyn and near to the water wheel stood the Smithy, which is believed to be the oldest building on the site, and where the drills for blasting holes in the rock were made and sharpened. The men used to make a shilling or two (5p or 10p) from here by selling cups of tea to visitors on their way up the mountain. Enterprising lot those miners, I wonder if the foreman knew about it?

Between the 1750s and 1913 there were quite a number of mines on Snowdon, some were successful, while others barely survived. Glaslyn is the best known mining area but it is not the only one. A number of copper mines existed on the slopes above Nant Gwynant and to the north above Llanberis. The Clogwyn Mine, situated below the Clogwyn Station near Llyn Du'r Arddu, was the first mine to be opened up on Snowdon. Nor was copper the only material to be mined, many tons of lead were also fetched out.

But the one industry which really came into its own in this area and for over 200 years brought prosperity (for the owners at least!) and work for the people of villages for miles around was slate.

Entering the village of Llanberis in the 19th century you would have been confronted by a narrow High Street with small dismal cottages on each side. Here and there would be much larger houses belonging to the managers of the quarries and local business men. The street would be bustling with locals—women in their long skirts and shawls, men in large boots or clogs, clay pipe in mouth on their way to the quarries to start their long gruelling day.

There were a few pubs and of course more chapels, as the Welsh were, and still are, a very religious people. The largest hotel was 'The Victoria Hotel', which would later become the 'Royal Victoria Hotel' after Queen Victoria's visit to the area in 1887 during her tour of the country to celebrate her Golden Anniversary.

In many ways the village hasn't changed all that much in the last hundred years, the High Street is wider and the houses in the village today are modern and very well kept, although some of the old terrace houses are still to be seen.

The two lakes, Llyn Padarn and Llyn Peris dominate the area, and between them standing above the village on a rocky spur are the re-mains of Dolbadarn Castle, guarding the Llanberis Pass, as it has for hundreds of years. Here in the heartland of his realm, Prince Llewelyn the Great of Gwynedd built it's mighty round tower and keep in 1230 – 40. The castle was little used after Edward I's conquest of Gwynedd in 1282, but it is easy to imagine local children playing in the remains during their short childhood before they would be forced to start work

Slate mining underground in 1910

at about six years of age to help support the family. That was until the introduction of the 1870 Education Act which made it compulsory for all children between the ages of five and 13 to attend school and receive at least an elementary education.

The largest user of labour here was of course the slate quarry, namely the Vivian and Dinorwic Quarries. These open quarries were developed in tiers 20 metres high (about 60 to 70 feet), which in time covered the whole of the mountainside (Elidir Fawr) across the lake from Llanberis.

The very first quarry worked by the terrace method was Penrhyn Quarry at Bethesda in 1782; the Dinorwic Quarry was opened in 1809 by Thomas Asheton Smith. This quarry developed very quickly until there were 3,000 people working there in 1898 – 1900, and the terraces had reached the height of 915 metres (3,000 feet) above sea level.

During the early years at Dinorwic, hand tools were used to remove large slabs off the rock face. The men would push a long chisel-ended tool back and forth until they had made a powder hole which would then be filled with black powder for blasting. The blasting dislodged

Quarrymen's 'cottages' where they would spend the week

large rectangular blocks which would then have to be split into slabs capable of being transported to the dressing mills called 'Sheds'.

Large saws were used to cut the slate into smaller sections which would then be split by hand into thinner pieces (slates for roofs). Splitting these slates was a skilled job and showed the craftsmanship of the quarrymen.

During the 19th century demand for Welsh slate came from the fast growing industrial towns in this country, Europe and the U.S.A. To meet this demand, a harbour was built between Bangor and Caernarfon on the Menai Straits called Porth Dinorwic.

In the early days, the slates were transported overland to Caernarfon for shipment abroad. These were first ferried across Llyn Padarn, but from 1824 they were taken by horse drawn tramways between the quarry and Porth Dinorwic. From 1842 a new railway, known locally as the 'Padarn Railway' (it's real name was Dinorwic Slate Quarry Railway), operated down the northern shore of Llyn Padarn and on through the valley of Afon Rhythallt until it reached a point just east of Porth Dinorwic. From here the slates came down to the harbour by way of an incline. One of the trains which operated on this line was called *'Fire Queen'*, and worked the line until 1886. She is preserved today in the Railway Museum at Penrhyn Castle which is looked after by the National Trust.

It's true to say that the slate quarry was the main artery of the village of Llanberis and for many miles around it was the main employer. The quarry had it's workshops, iron and brass foundry, saw mills—in fact it was completely self contained, and in the event of accidents—and there were many—they even had their own hospital which you can see on Allt Ddu on the eastern shore of Llyn Padarn.

Responsibility for the hospital was for many years in the hands of Doctor R.H. Mills Roberts, FRCS, who was, by all accounts, a remarkable man. He was surgeon, doctor, and even dentist all rolled into one.

It's not often that you hear of a surgeon and a blacksmith forming a professional partnership, but Dr Mills Roberts did and many of the splints, the operating table, artificial limbs etc. were made by the cooperation of both men.

I came across a story of how a man was injured so badly in an accident in the quarry that both his arms had to be amputated, one at the shoulder and the other lower down. The blacksmith in partnership with the good Doctor made a device which enabled the injured man to use a spoon and a knife to eat, and even more importantly, enabled him to take his cap off before going into Chapel.

A few years ago I had been walking the zig zags in the woods above the hospital which gives you a good view of the terrace system and how it worked. On coming down it suddenly started to rain quite heavily, and seeing a small building ahead with the door open I went inside to shelter. As I looked around the building however, I realised I had wondered into the mortuary. Looking at the two slate slabs resting on brick plinths, I wondered what stories they could tell. I was certainly pleased when the rain stopped and I could continue my walk.

The Dinorwic Quarry, though important to Llanberis is not situated on Snowdon. But Snowdon did have its slate quarries. A large operation

A photograph of the summit thought to have been taken in the 1870s

existed in Cwm Llan on the south side of the mountain where Victorian visitors would have made their way through the workings on their way up the mountain. I wonder what the workers thought of these strange people who came to the scene of their hard work for pleasure?

Smaller workings also existed on the mountain's western slopes above Rhyd Ddu and on the bwlch between Yr Wyddfa and Yr Aran.

But a new industry had been developing on Snowdon. Throughout the 19th century Snowdon saw a steady rise in the number of tourists each year. By tourists I don't mean ordinary men and women, but what we would consider to be 'middle class', i.e. people in trade or of independent means. Many of these visitors wanted to ascend the highest mountain in Wales having been inspired by the writings of travellers like Thomas Pennant and George Borrow. Local people soon realised that a living could be made by catering to the needs of these visitors.

This 'tourist trade' became for many a lifeline. Remember that in the 19th century there was no state pension, or compensation for loss of job through illness or injury. If the quarryman lost his job he had to rely on other family members (hence the large families) or he would be forced to seek help from the parish or Workhouse. Providing accommodation and refreshments for those who came to explore Snowdon was far less dangerous than working in the quarries and mines. Also the miners and farmers knew the mountains well and thus made ideal guides. They could earn as much as three shillings (15p) a day for their services. Thomas Pennant, one of the earliest travellers to record his impressions of North Wales hired one such guide by the name of Hugh Shone for an ascent of the mountain from Llanberis as early as 1786. On the summit he reported a 'circular wall of loose stones, within which travellers usually take their repast.' Throughout the 19th century guides were readily available to accompany wealthy travellers to the summit. George Borrow hired a guide to accompany himself and his daughter Henrietta to the summit in the 1860s and wrote an account of the ascent in his famous book, *'Wild Wales'*.

As I mentioned earlier, miners were supplying hot drinks and food for walkers on their way up Snowdon quite early in the 19th century. One such man, was Morris Williams from Amlwch and in 1838 he built the

An early postcard sent from the summit

first hut on the summit, just below the cairn. It had thick stone walls, and inner walls lined with wooden boards. I call this first building a hut as it couldn't by any means be described as a 'hotel'.

The first hotel was built two years later in 1840 and consisted of two huts which belonged to the owners of 'The Victoria Hotel' down in Llanberis. Later still, larger and more robust buildings were erected and those who wished to watch the sun rise from the summit could make their way up in the evening, have a meal, rest, and enjoy breakfast for the tidy sum of 8 shillings (40p). George Borrow recorded his impression of the summit 'hotel' in this way: 'The Wyddfa (the summit cairn) is about thirty feet in diameter and is surrounded on three sides by a low wall. In the middle of it is a rude cabin, in which refreshments are sold and in which a person resides through the year.'

By the early 1900s a larger chalet-style hotel occupied the summit and was advertised as 'The highest hotel in the Kingdom'. This building can be seen in many photographs from the period and became quite a landmark before it was demolished in 1923 to make way for a new summit station. The recently demolished summit station and cafe was built in 1936 and was designed by Sir Clough Williams-Ellis of Porthmeirion fame.

One of the most important dates for Snowdon during the 19th century was April 4th 1896, when the train made it's maiden journey to the summit. Unfortunately the engine ('**Ladas**') left the track on it's return journey just beyond the Clogwyn Station (this is the bridge you will go under when walking the Llanberis Path) and plunged into Cwm Glas Bach above the Llanberis Pass. The driver and fireman managed to jump free and the brakes were applied to the carriages avoiding disaster. There was just one fatality—Mr Ellis Roberts the proprietor of the 'Padarn Villa Hotel'. He had also tried to jump from the carriages and sustained series injuries. His leg was amputated but he died later that night.

This journey had taken two years hard planning to bring about, although plans to build a railway to the summit had first been discussed way back in the 1870s. It had been conceived as a way of enabling Llanberis to remain the main centre for ascending Snowdon. Beddgelert, on the southern side of the mountain, had become a serious rival with many locals providing their services as guides. The building of the North Wales Narrow Gauge Railway linking Beddgelert to Caernarfon with a new station at Rhyd Ddu called the 'Snowdon Station' had already taken many visitors away from Llanberis. Beddgelert even had its own route to the summit known as the 'Beddgelert Path'. This is now the Rhyd Ddu Path but it started from a point further south known as 'Pitt's Head' which could be reached by train from Beddgelert. But with the building of the Snowdon Mountain Railway Llanberis won the day and has remained the main centre for ascending Snowdon.

Mara Books & Northern Eye Books

www.marabooks.co.uk or www.northerneyebooks.co.uk

Mara Books publish a range of walking books for Cheshire and North Wales and have the following list to date. A complete list of current titles is available on our web site.

North Wales
Mountain walking
Mountain & Hill Walking in Snowdonia

This is a two-volume in-depth guide to every summit of note in the Snowdonia National Park.

Volume 1 – Carneddau, Glyderau, Snowdon and Eifionydd.
ISBN 978 1 902512 18 1.

Volume 2 – Moelwynion, Rhinogydd, Arenig, Arans, Dyfi hills and Cadair Idris as well as the Tarrens and Berwyns.
ISBN 978 1 902512 22 8.

Snowdonia's best Mountain Walks

ISBN 978 1 902512 19 8. A book which gathers the very best walks and scrambles to be enjoyed throughout the Snowdonia National Park, with at least one walk in all the main hill groups.

Leisure walking
Coastal Walks around Anglesey

ISBN 978 1 902512 20 4. A collection of circular walks which explore the varied scenery of Anglesey's beautiful coastline, designated an Area of Outstanding Natural Beauty.

The Isle of Anglesey Coastal Path – The Official Guide

ISBN 978 1 902512 13 6. A guide to the 125-mile circuit of Anglesey's stunning coast, an Area of Outstanding Natural Beauty.

Walking in the Conwy Valley

ISBN 978 0 9522409 7 6. A collection of circular walks exploring the varied scenery of this beautiful valley from the Great Orme to Betws-y-coed.

Walks on the Lleyn Peninsula

ISBN 978 1 902512 00 6. A collection of circular walks which explore both the wild and beautiful coastline and hills of the Lleyn Peninsula.

Walking in the Clwydian Range

ISBN 978 1 902512 14 3. A collection of 21 circular walks in the Clwydian Range Area of Outstanding Natural Beauty.

Walking in the Vale of Clwyd and Hiraethog

ISBN 978 0 9559625 3 0. A collection of circular walks exploring the undiscovered country between the Clwydian Range and the Conwy Valley.

Walking in northern Snowdonia

ISBN 978 1 902512 06 8. Twenty circular walks exploring the beautiful and dramatic valleys in the northern half of the Snowdonia National Park.

Mountaineering

The Mountain Men

ISBN 978 1 902512 11 2. This book tells the story of the pioneer rock climbers in Snowdonia in the closing decades of the nineteenth century until the outbreak of World War I.

The Day the Rope Broke

ISBN 978-1-902512-12-9. The story of the first ascent of the Matterhorn by the Victorian mountaineer Edward Whymper and the disaster which followed. Illustrated in colour and black and white.

Some common Welsh place name elements found in the Snowdon area and their meaning:

Afon *(a-von)*	river
Allt *(al-th-t)*	slope
Bedd *(beth)*	grave
Bwlch *(bul-k)*	pass
Bychan *(buc-an)*	small
Clogwyn	crag/cliff
Crib/Gribin	ridge
Cwm *(coom)*	glacial valley
Ddu/Du *(thee, dee)*	black
Ddysgl *(this-gul)*	dish
Dyffryn	valley
Fach/Bach *(vach)*	small
Fawr/Mawr *(vaw-r)*	large
Glas	green, blue
Goch	red
Graig/Craig	crag
Gwastad	plain, level
Llan	church
Moel *(moy-l)*	bald or rounded hill
Mynydd *(mun-uth)*	mountain
Nant	stream
Pen	head
Rhyd	ford
Saethau	to shoot, arrows
Wen, gwyn	white